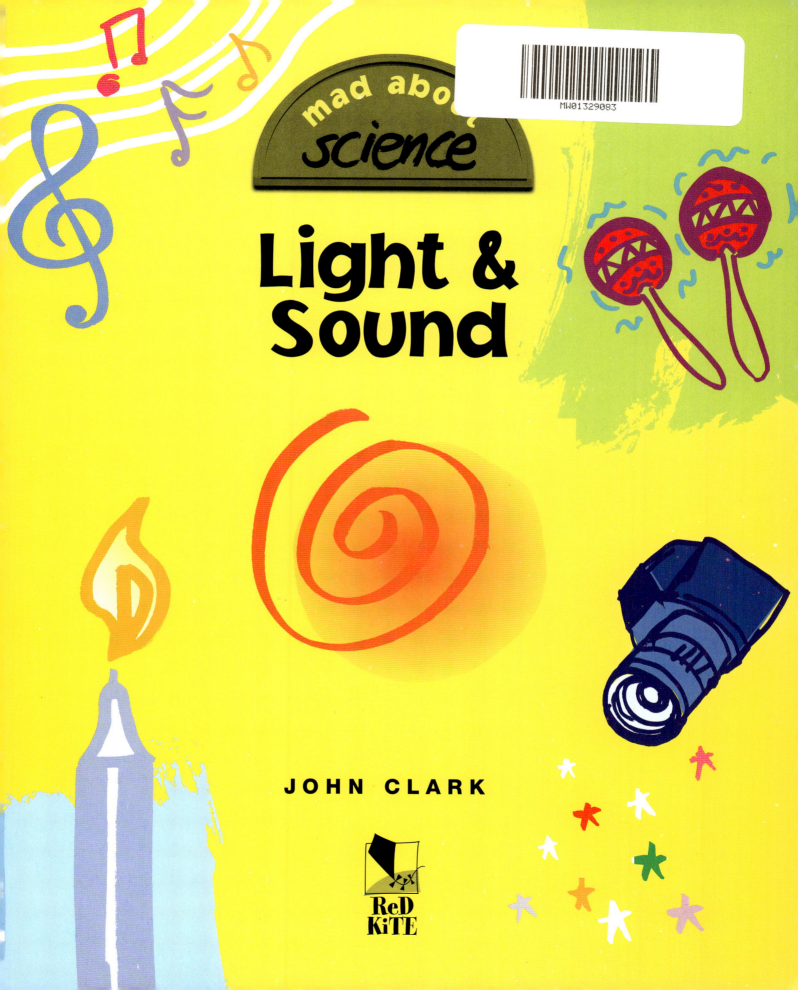

mad about science

Light & Sound

JOHN CLARK

ReD KiTE

Welcome to Mad About Science: Light & Sound!

Do you know how an eclipse happens or why some watches glow in the dark? Could you explain how your voice works, or why you have two eyes instead of one? With a range of exciting and fun experiments, amazing facts and colourful illustrations, this book is a fascinating guide to light, reflections, colours and shadows, as well as explaining how sounds are made, why some sounds are quiet and some loud, how your ears work and much more.

Throughout the book, you will find experiments and activities that are great fun and easy to do. Discover how to make a periscope, how to tell the time using the Sun, and how to find your blind spot. Most of the things that you will need for them can be found in your home. Follow the instructions for each experiment carefully and always take care when you are using sharp tools and knives.

If you want to know about a particular subject, just look it up in the index at the back of the book. Otherwise, simply turn to page 4 and have fun!

Note: The experiments described in this book are designed to be safe and easy to carry out at home. The author and publishers can accept no responsibility for any accidents that occur as a result of using the book. If in doubt, consult an adult.

Contents

Let There be Light! 4
Making Shadows 6
Mirror Images 8
Round the Bend! 10
Rainbow Colours 12
Seeing the Light 14
Illusions and Images 16
Good Vibrations 18
Speedy Sound 20
How Loud? 22
High or Low? 24
All Ears 26
Echo Effects 28
Making Waves 30
Glossary 31
Index 32

First published in the UK in 2001 by Red Kite Books,
an imprint of Haldane Mason Ltd, PO Box 34196, London NW10 3YB.
www.redkitebooks.net

Reprinted 2007
Hardback edition published 2006

Copyright © Haldane Mason Ltd, 2001

All rights reserved. No part of this publication may be reproduced, stored
in a retrieval system or transmitted in any form or by any means, electronic,
mechanical, photocopying, recording, or otherwise, without the prior
permission of the copyright holder.

Hardback ISBN: 978-1-905339-11-2
Paperback ISBN: 978-1-905339-07-5

Printed in China

British Library CIP Data: a catalogue record for
this title is available from the British Library

A HALDANE MASON BOOK
Project Editor: Kate Latham
Editor: Anna Claybourne
Designer: Rachel Clark
Illustrations: Phil Ford and Peter Bull Studios
Educational Consultant: John Stringer BSc

Picture Acknowledgements
Bruce Coleman Collection 12, /Peter Hinchliffe 5;
Mary Evans Picture Library 21; **Image Bank** 6, 8, 19, 22, 25, 29;
Oxford Scientific Photos /Daniel Cox 27, /David Dennis 10,
/Mike Linley/Survival Anglia 15b; **Premaphotos** 15t.

Light & Sound

Let There be Light!

Everyone knows about light. It comes from the Sun, from light bulbs, candles, street lamps and car headlights, and it surrounds us most of the time. But what exactly is it? In fact, light is a type of energy – just like heat, electricity, movement and sound. Unlike other forms of energy, we can see light. And without it, we can't see a thing!

Where's it from?

During the daytime, most of the light around you comes from the Sun. As well as helping you to see, sunlight is good for you. Your body uses it to make vitamin D, which makes your bones stronger. It also provides warmth – which is particularly useful when you want to dry off on the beach after a swim. Plants need sunlight too, because they use it to make food. Inside a plant's leaves, water from the soil and carbon dioxide (a type of gas) from the air combine to make the food chemicals the plant needs to grow and be healthy. Energy from sunlight is used to power this chemical reaction, which is called photosynthesis, meaning 'making with light'.

Of course, it's not always sunny – sometimes it's dark (you'll find out why later). Then, we have to make our own light by turning other kinds of energy into light energy. The earliest lamps were candles and oil lamps. They work by burning fuel, such as wax or oil, which contain chemical energy that came from the Sun. As they burn, this turns into light energy, and the candle burns or lamp glows. It also gives off heat energy, which is why candles and lamps are hot to the touch. We still use candles, but nowadays we rely more on electric lights. Inside a light bulb, electrical energy heats a very thin piece of metal until it is white hot and gives off light. The light in a fluorescent tube or a TV screen comes from phosphors – chemicals that glow when energy flows through them.

Candles, light bulbs and phosphors are all light sources.

Did you know?

Some watches have hands that glow in the dark. You can also buy glow-in-the-dark stars to stick on your ceiling. How do they work? The answer is luminescence (which simply means 'shining'). They contain special chemicals which soak up light during the day, then release it when it's dark. Some animals, including fireflies, glow-worms and some types of fish, are 'bioluminescent' – which means they can glow in the dark, too. Their bodies contain chemicals that react with each other to give off light. Unlike most other ways of making light, this does not give off heat energy. This is just as well, or fireflies would cook themselves!

Glow-worms attract food by glowing in the dark.

Try this!

Energy race

This experiment shows that light travels faster than sound. You will need a couple of objects to bang together, such as two pan lids. Ask a friend to stand about 20–30m away from you, facing you. Now get your friend to bang the two objects together. You will see the action before you hear it! When you see an object, light bounces off it and into your eyes. The light zooms from your friend to you super-fast – at the speed of light, in fact! However, it will be a fraction of a second before you hear the clang. This is because sound travels more slowly than light.

Amazing fact

The energy that falls on the Earth as sunlight takes about ten million years to get from the centre of the Sun to the Earth. The last part of its journey – from the outer parts of the Sun to us – takes just eight and a half minutes.

Light & Sound

Making Shadows

One of the most important things to know about light is that it travels in straight lines. This is how light makes shadows. Instead of curving around an object, light shines straight past it, making a shadow of the object where the light couldn't get through. This is why your shadow on the ground or a wall is the same shape as you.

In the shadows

When you're in a shadow, it means there's something between you and a light source, such as the Sun. The biggest example of this is night-time, which is a kind of giant shadow. At night, your part of the Earth is facing away from the Sun. The Sun is still shining, but the light hits the other side of the Earth and zooms straight past it, out into space. The side facing away from the Sun is left in shadowy darkness.

Opaque or transparent?

Objects cast shadows because light cannot pass through them. In other words, they are opaque. When light hits an opaque object, it either bounces off or is absorbed (soaked up) into the object. Shiny objects, such as mirrors, make lots of light reflect (bounce) off them. Rough, dark objects, like a piece of black cloth, absorb most of the light that hits them. Other objects, like your body, reflect some light and absorb the rest.

But not all objects are opaque. If they were, our windows and spectacles wouldn't be much use! Transparent substances such as glass and clear plastic let light shine right through them. So they don't have a dark shadow, like opaque objects do. Plane glass, like glass in normal windows which we can see through, is perfectly flat on both sides. But if one side is roughened or embossed with a pattern, it scatters the light. It still lets light through, but you can't see through it clearly. That's why it's often used for bathroom windows.

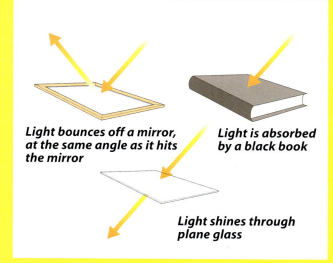

Light bounces off a mirror, at the same angle as it hits the mirror

Light is absorbed by a black book

Light shines through plane glass

Making shadows

In a solar eclipse, the Moon casts its shadow on the Earth. Where the Sun is fully hidden is called the umbra of the eclipse. The larger shadow, the penumbra, is where part of the Sun is visible.

Did you know?

An eclipse happens when the Sun, the Moon and the Earth line up in space. In a solar eclipse, the Moon moves between the Earth and the Sun. The Moon blocks out light from the Sun, making a huge shadow fall across the Earth. If you are standing right in the middle of this shadow, you see a total eclipse, and it's almost as dark as night-time.

Amazing fact

If you were standing in a shadow on the planet Mercury, you would be more than 600°C colder than if you were standing in direct sunlight. Brrrrr!

Try this! Make a sundial

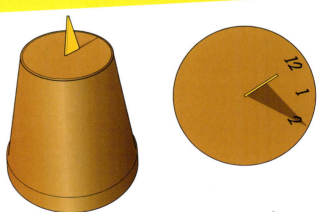

A sundial is one of the oldest ways of telling the time, using shadows cast by the Sun. To make a sundial you'll need a right-angled triangle with sides of 8cm, made of stiff cardboard, some sticky tape and a large plant pot. Turn the plant pot upside-down and tape the triangle upright on to the base of the pot. At 12 noon on a sunny day, turn your sundial so that the triangle casts only a thin line of shadow. Use a felt-tip pen to mark this position and label it '12'. Leave the pot in the same position, and label the positions of the shadow at 1 o'clock, 2 o'clock, and so on. The following morning (if it's still sunny!) you can mark the positions of the shadows corresponding to the morning hours. Once you've marked all the daylight hours, you can use your sundial as a clock during the day.

Mirror Images

We see some objects because they give off light. But we see most things because light bounces off them into our eyes. Some surfaces reflect light better than others – a mirror reflects light completely and so we see an image of what is directly in front of the mirror. Or do we?

Seeing is believing

The image in a flat or plane mirror is the same size as the reflected object, but reversed left to right. If you look at your reflection and wink your right eye, the reflection winks its left eye. Objects reversed in this way are called – surprise, surprise – mirror images.

The images in curved mirrors are different. A mirror that curves outwards is called a convex mirror. It gives a wide view with a small image that is the right way up. The rear-view mirror in a car is a convex mirror. A concave mirror curves inwards. Distant objects are reflected to give a smaller, upside-down image. But objects that are close to the mirror appear the right way up and bigger. So concave mirrors are used for shaving mirrors. You can see these different reflections if you look at the back (convex) and the inside (concave) of the bowl of a polished metal spoon.

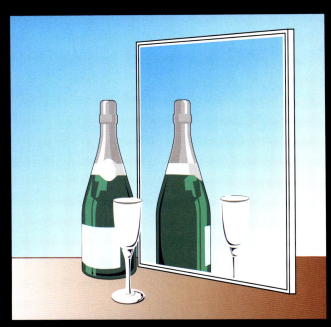

With a plane mirror, the object is the same distance in front of the mirror as the image appears 'behind' the mirror.

Did you know?

If you've ever been into a hall of mirrors at a fairground, you'll have seen some pretty strange reflections! They are made using a combination of convex and concave surfaces in the same mirror. The convex parts make you look smaller, while the concave parts make you look bigger. Together, they make you look like something from another planet!

Mirror Images

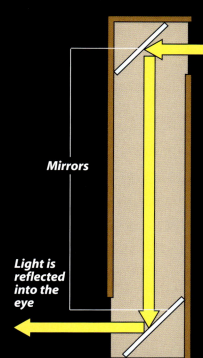

Mirrors

Light is reflected into the eye

Try this! See round corners

A periscope is a device that uses mirrors to help you see round corners or over walls. Submarines have periscopes so that people inside the submarine can scan the sea surface for danger. To make a simple periscope you'll need a long, narrow cardboard box (the kind you get kitchen foil in will do, but make sure it's empty first), two small mirrors, scissors and tape. Tape the two mirrors into the box as shown here – they must face each other at exactly the same angle. Then tape the box shut and cut out holes opposite each mirror. You use the periscope by looking into one of the holes. The mirrors should let you see out of the other hole.

Ghostly glass

Plane glass is transparent, but its surface reflects some light, so it can also act as a mirror. You've probably seen your reflection in a shop window, for example. By using reflections, a large piece of plane glass can be used to put a ghost on the stage! The audience sees the actors on the stage through a large piece of glass while a mirror is used to reflect the image of an actor playing a ghost on to the glass. The actor is really underneath the stage, out of sight of the audience.

Amazing fact

Scientists have measured how far it is to the Moon by reflecting light from a laser off a mirror which was placed on the Moon by astronauts. Knowing how fast light travels, the time that the light took to bounce back told them the exact distance to the Moon.

Try this! Making mirrors

Take a piece of new kitchen foil and smooth it carefully. The bright side makes a fairly good mirror. Nearly all the light that hits the foil is reflected in the same direction, but if you crumple the foil into a ball and then flatten it out again, it makes a very poor mirror. Why? The foil itself has not changed and it is still reflecting the same amount of light, but the reflective surface now consists of lots of small mirrors at different angles that reflect the light in different directions. Good mirrors have a perfectly flat surface, which is why most of them are made of glass.

Light & Sound

Round the Bend!

Light always travels in straight lines, but it can change direction if it is reflected from a surface. Surprisingly, light also changes direction when it shines through something transparent, such as glass or water. This is called refraction, and it's very useful – it makes lenses in spectacles, telescopes and microscopes work.

Bendy light

When a beam of light passes through a piece of glass or into water, it slows down very slightly. If the light enters at an angle, slowing down makes it change direction, and the beam is bent.

But why does slowing down make the beam bend? To understand this, imagine an army of soldiers marching in rows of three. If they march at an angle off smooth ground on to a ploughed field, the soldiers who step on the soil first will have to slow down before the others. So for a few steps, one end of the row will go faster than the other, and the group will swing round.

The straw seems to change size and shape as the reflected light is refracted by the glass and then by both the glass and the coloured water.

Try this! Bending light

You'll need a torch, a piece of cardboard, some scissors and a glass bottle filled with water and a few drops of milk. In a darkened room, make a beam of light by shining the torch through a narrow slit in the piece of cardboard. Shine it through the glass bottle filled with milky water to see how the glass and water bend (refract) and scatter the light.

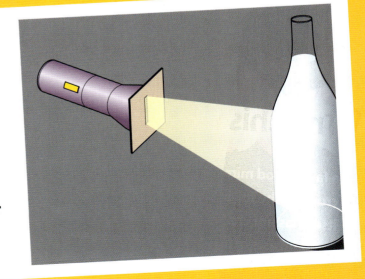

Round the Bend!

Lens control

We can control the way light bends by giving the surfaces of a piece of glass a curved shape. A curved piece of glass like this is called a lens (Latin for lentil, because that's what some lenses look like). There are two main kinds. A lens with the surfaces curved outwards is called a convex (or converging) lens. Parallel rays of light passing through it are brought together so that they converge to a focus. A magnifying glass is a kind of convex lens. It bends rays of light so that when you look through the glass, objects look bigger. A lens with its surfaces curved inwards is a concave lens. It makes parallel light rays move apart or diverge. Objects seen through a concave (or diverging) lens appear smaller than they really are. Both types of lenses are used in spectacles, cameras and optical instruments such as telescopes and microscopes.

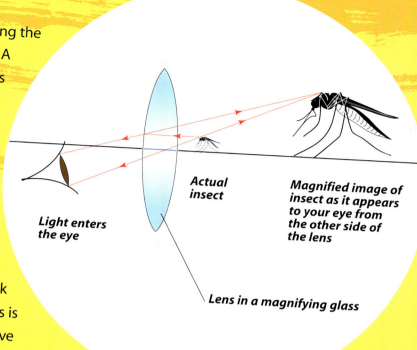

An insect seen through a magnifying glass is magnified as the convex lens bends the light rays.

Amazing fact

Giant objects in space have a strong enough pull of gravity to bend light rays. Stars are sources of both heat and light. The light from stars normally travels in straight lines, but if this light passes close to a galaxy or a group of galaxies which contain billions of stars, its enormous pull of gravity bends the passing light rays just like light bends when it travels through a lens. This effect is called a gravitational lens.

Did you know?

The first simple microscope was made in the 1700s by the Dutchman Anton van Leeuwenhoek (pronounced lay-ven-hook). It had a tiny single convex lens, which Leeuwenhoek made by grinding down a bead of glass, but it was powerful enough to see blood cells and bacteria. Modern microscopes have several lenses.

Light & Sound

Rainbow Colours

Light often appears to be colourless, but sunlight is actually made up of a range of different colours. If that sounds unlikely, think about a rainbow in the sky. Rainbows are made of pure sunlight.

Refracting rainbow

A rainbow is a special example of refraction. You see the colours because when sunlight shines through raindrops, it bends. But the drops of water bend some of the colours that sunlight is made from more than others. This makes the rays of light spread out into the colours of the rainbow.

Can you see seven colours in this rainbow? You should see red, orange, yellow, green, blue, indigo and violet.

Spectrum magic

In about 1665 the English scientist Isaac Newton made an artificial rainbow by passing a beam of sunlight through a prism (a solid glass shape). The prism bent each colour of light a different amount. The result is millions of coloured bands, called a spectrum, which follow the colours of a rainbow. Newton recognized the spectrum as being made up of seven main colours: red, orange, yellow, green, blue, indigo (dark blue) and violet (purple).

When light from the Sun is reflected inside raindrops, the drops act like individual prisms and split the light into rainbow colours.

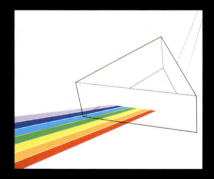

Light is split into a spectrum of colours by a prism.

Seeing red

So, when 'white' sunlight hits an object, it actually shines all the colours of the rainbow on to it. But why does a red book look red? What happens is that the book absorbs all of the rainbow colours in sunlight except red. Only red is reflected back to our eyes and that is the colour we see. The same is true for green objects, blue ones, or any other colour. Black objects absorb all the light rays, so none are reflected back into our eyes, and white objects reflect all of the light rays.

Rainbow Colours

Try this! Make a rainbow

You can make your very own rainbow or spectrum by using a bowl of water and a small mirror. Fill a bowl or shallow dish with about 3–4cm of water. Now hold the mirror at an angle so that the Sun shines on to it below the surface of the water. The Sun's rays will be reflected at an angle. Now hold a piece of white paper to 'catch' the reflected Sun. Can you see a rainbow? Warning: do not look directly at the reflection of the Sun in the mirror or you will damage your eyes.

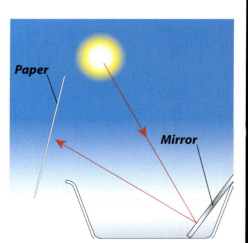

Did you know?

Colour filters let through only one colour of light. Any transparent, coloured substance can act as a filter – try looking through coloured sweet wrappings or one side of a pair of 3–D glasses. If you look at a white cloud through a filter, the cloud takes on the colour of the filter. The whole spectrum of colours will be reflected but the filter will only let the one colour through. But if you look at a coloured object, such as a green book cover, its colour will change depending on the colour of your filter. Through a red filter, it will look black, because the red won't let the reflected green light through.

Amazing fact

Although light has many colours, it is made up of three main or 'primary' colours – red, green and blue. Any other colour can be made from a mixture of these three. This is how a television set produces a colour picture. The picture that appears on the screen is made up of tiny dots of red, green and blue light. In different mixtures, these three colours create the shades making up the picture.

Try this! Mixing colours

You know that white light can be split into the colours of the rainbow. But you can also mix the colours to turn them back into white. You will need a circle of white card, about 10cm across, and a pencil. Divide the card into seven segments and colour them red, orange, yellow, blue, green, indigo and violet. Push the pencil through the centre of the card and spin it like a spinning top. If you can spin it fast enough, the colours will combine and the circle will look greyish-white. (You will notice that the edges of the card look whiter than the centre – this is because the edges of the card spin faster than the centre of the card.)

Light & Sound

Seeing the Light

Eyes can see things because they 'collect' light from objects. Objects either give off their own light, or reflect light from another light source. Your eyes detect the light and turn it into nerve messages that go to your brain. Finally, your brain converts them into images in your mind. So your sense of sight depends on your eyes and your brain working together.

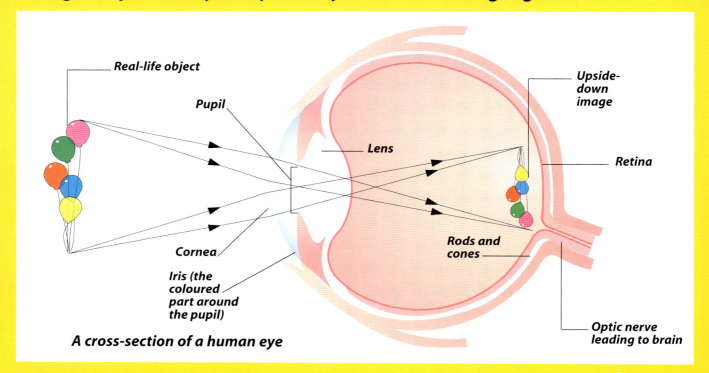

A cross-section of a human eye

Camera eyes

The human eye is constructed like a camera (although eyes came before cameras, so it's really the other way round). Light enters the eye through a window at the front of the eyeball called the cornea. It then passes through the pupil, the black hole at the centre of the eye.

The lens inside the eye focuses light rays on to the light-sensitive retina at the back of the eye. Cells called rods and cones cover the retina. These cells trigger nerve impulses when they are struck by light. The nerve impulses pass along the optic nerve to the brain, where they are interpreted as images.

The brain also has another job to do. If you have used a magnifying glass to focus an image on a piece of paper, you'll know that the image appears on the paper upside-down. So do the images at the back of the eye. Fortunately, our brain turns them the right way up without us having to tell it to do this.

Seeing the Light

Did you know?

Many insects, such as flies and butterflies, appear to have two eyes, just like humans. But instead of single lenses like ours, their eyes are made up of thousands of tubes, bundled together like straws, and at the end of each tube is a tiny lens. These are called compound eyes, and they allow insects to see all around them, which is why it is so difficult to catch a fly.

Horse flies use their huge compound eyes to locate juicy, blood-filled animals.

Try this! Seeing colour

The light-sensing cells called rods, which are mostly around the edge of the retina, detect black, white and grey. The cones detect colour, and are in the middle of the retina. In a room with dim lighting, hold up a coloured object at the side of a friend's head, while they look forward. Can they tell what colour it is? Move the object slowly round until it is in front of their eyes. When could they see its colour?

3-D vision

Having two eyes a slight distance apart helps to give you 3-D vision – scientists call it stereoscopic vision. Each eye sees a slightly different view, and the brain combines the different images to work out how far away an object is. Try closing one eye and looking around an unfamiliar room or scene. It's much more difficult to work out how far away things are with only one eye. Don't even try pouring a glass of water!

Amazing fact

The human eye can see 10 million different colours, but some creatures can see beyond the ends of the rainbow of colours that we see. Snakes that home in on the body warmth of their prey can see heat rays that are invisible to us. And some butterflies and bees can see ultraviolet light, also invisible to us, that is reflected by many flowers.

The Brimstone butterfly has special patterns on its wings to attract other butterflies who can see ultraviolet light.

Light & Sound

Illusions and Images

The brain has a big part to play in producing the images we see. It has to interpret nerve impulses from the eye to create the image that we automatically see. But the brain can easily be fooled, especially if the eyes give it one message when it is expecting another. Tricks called optical illusions can deceive your brain into seeing something that's not there, but they do help you to understand how your vision really works.

Blind spot

The optic nerve, which carries nerve impulses from the eye to the brain, joins the eye at a place near the middle of the retina (you can see this on the diagram on page 14). There are no light-detecting rods or cones at this spot on the back of the eye, and for this reason it is called the blind spot. You don't normally notice this gap in your vision because the brain cleverly 'fills in' the missing information from the images surrounding the blind spot.

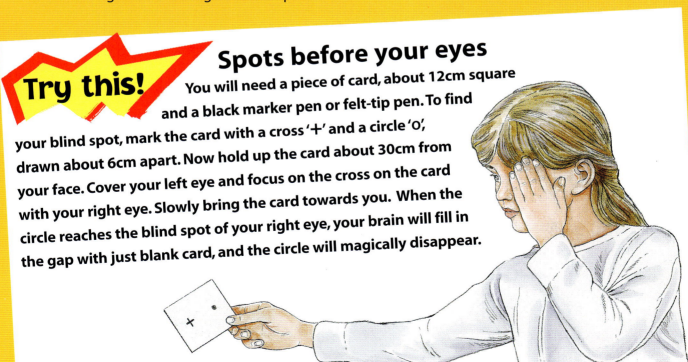

Try this!

Spots before your eyes

You will need a piece of card, about 12cm square and a black marker pen or felt-tip pen. To find your blind spot, mark the card with a cross '+' and a circle 'O', drawn about 6cm apart. Now hold up the card about 30cm from your face. Cover your left eye and focus on the cross on the card with your right eye. Slowly bring the card towards you. When the circle reaches the blind spot of your right eye, your brain will fill in the gap with just blank card, and the circle will magically disappear.

Illusions and Images

Try this!

Optical illusions

Try fooling your brain with the optical illusions here. You'll find that your brain makes all kinds of assumptions about what it can see – even when it's wrong!

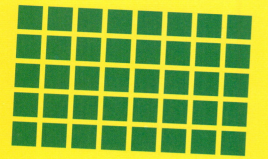

If you stare at this grid, you can see paler green small squares between the large squares – but they're not really there.

Look at this goblet. Can you see the two people who would drink from it?

Look at the two small horizontal lines. Which is the longer? Now measure them to see if you are right.

Did you know?

A camera is very like a human eye. It is a light-tight box with a lens at the front that focuses light on to a film at the back of the camera. A diaphragm (like the iris in the eye) opens and closes a hole (like the pupil) to control the amount of light entering the camera. A shutter opens just long enough to let enough light in to take the picture. The photographer focuses the lens by moving it in and out (unlike the lens in the eye, which focuses by changing its thickness). As in the eye, the image on the film is upside-down, but we can easily solve that by turning our photos the right way up!

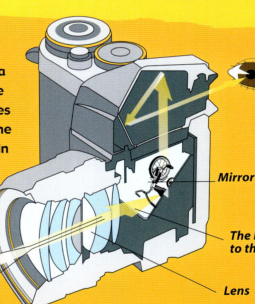

Mirror

The light's path to the eye

Lens

Amazing fact

If we watch a series of images in rapid succession, there is a slight delay before one image fades in the brain to be replaced by the next one. This is called persistence of vision, and it's crucial to how films and television work. The movements we see on screen are really an illusion. We actually see 24–30 stationary images per second, but our brain 'hangs on' to one image before receiving the next, so it looks like continuous movement.

Light & Sound

Good Vibrations

Just like light, sound is a kind of energy – energy you can hear rather than see. Sound travels through the air as a series of vibrations called sound waves. It can also travel through liquids and solids. Unlike light, sound can't travel millions of miles across empty space. It must have air, water or another substance to move through as a vibration.

Noise or notes?

Sound energy is made when something vibrates, making the air around it vibrate too. For example, when you pluck a guitar string or bang a drum, it vibrates. The vibrations pass into the air, and travel to your ears. You can see a guitar string vibrate, but you can't always see sound vibrations – for example, when you clap your hands.

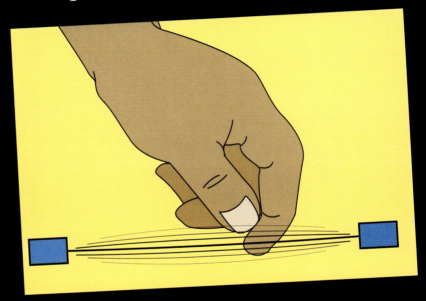

Hand clapping or banging two stones together makes a sound that scientists call 'noise'. Noise doesn't have any particular note, or pitch. But musical instruments produce sounds that do have pitch – you can hear the separate notes.

Amazing fact

Doctors are using sound to help broken bones heal faster. Directing sound waves at the ends of broken bones makes them form new bone nearly twice as fast as normal. This technique is given the grand name of Sonic Accelerated Fracture Healing.

Try this! Wineglass whine

You can amaze your friends by making a glass 'sing' with this trick. Take an empty wineglass and hold the base firmly on a tabletop. Lick one finger and rub it round and round the rim of the glass. It takes a little practice, but soon the glass will 'sing' with a pure, high note.

Good Vibrations

Try this!

Detecting sound waves

Sound waves travel through the air as vibrations. You can prove this by making your own sound detector. Take a glass bowl, a piece of clingfilm, an elastic band and some salt or sugar. Stretch the clingfilm tight across the top of the bowl to form a skin. Use the elastic band to hold it in place. Sprinkle a few grains of salt or sugar on the middle of the clingfilm. Now make a loud sound nearby by clapping your hands together. The sound vibrations in the air make the plastic skin vibrate, causing the salt crystals to jump up and down. You can prove that sound vibrations are made when you clap your hands even though you can't actually see them.

Making music

Instruments make musical sounds in three main ways. Stringed instruments have vibrating strings. These may be bowed to make them vibrate (as in a violin), plucked (as in a harp or guitar) or struck (as in a piano). In wind instruments, a vibrating column of air inside the instrument produces sound. The air is set in motion by a reed vibrating (as in an oboe or clarinet) or by the player's lips vibrating (as in a bugle or trumpet). And we all know that hitting something to make it vibrate produces sounds. You make music by banging the skins of drums, hitting the metal of a triangle or cymbals, or the strips of wood in a xylophone (although your parents might not call it music).

Did you know?

Although supersonic jet planes are very noisy, you can't hear one coming towards you! That's because it flies faster than the speed of sound, so it passes you before its sound arrives. When the sound does reach your ears, it is in the form of a shock wave that you hear as a loud bang – known as a sonic boom.

Light & Sound

Speedy Sound

Sound isn't as fast as light, but it's still fast. Sound waves travel through dry air at a speed of 343m/sec (metres per second). They travel even faster and farther through denser substances. In seawater they go at 1,500m/sec and in iron and steel at an amazing 5,000m/sec – a thousand times faster than a high-speed bullet.

Sound signals

Workers in tunnels and prisoners in jails make use of the fact that sound travels well in solids. They send signals to each other by tapping on metal pipes that run through the tunnel or prison. Hadrian's Wall in Scotland has clay pipes running along its length, and some historians think that the bored Roman soldiers patrolling the wall used to tap messages to each other in a similar way. Modern water engineers use the fact that sound vibrations travel well through metal by placing their ear at one end of a metal 'listening stick', with the other end on the ground, to listen out for water leaking out of underground pipes. And animals such as whales and dolphins make underwater cries that travel many kilometres at high speed, because sound travels that much faster in water than in air.

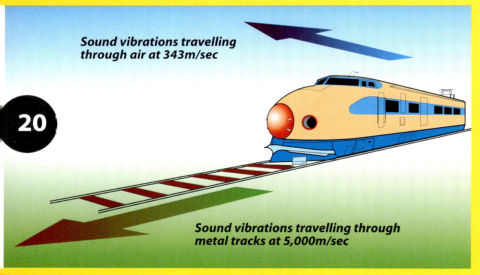

Sound vibrations travelling through air at 343m/sec

Sound vibrations travelling through metal tracks at 5,000m/sec

If you stand near a railway line, you can hear the rumble of an approaching train vibrating the rails long before you can hear the train itself.

Sound science

In 1705 the physicist William Derham climbed to the top of a church tower, taking a stopwatch with him. He had arranged for a helper to fire a cannon on a hilltop nearly 20km away. When he saw the flash of the cannon he started his watch, and then stopped it when he heard the bang. He now knew how long the sound had taken to travel 20km, and from this he could work out the speed of sound. He calculated it to be 348m/sec. Modern experiments have measured it at 343m/sec, so Derham was pretty close.

Speedy Sound

Try this!

Make a string telephone

You will need two empty tin cans or yoghurt pots, a length of string, a nail and a hammer. Use the nail and hammer to make a hole in the centre of the base of each can. Thread the string through the hole in one can and knot it on the inside. Thread the other end of the string through the hole in the other can, and knot it. Now get a friend to hold one can while you hold the other. Stretch the string tight and take it in turns to speak into the can. The speaker should have the can close to their mouth, and the listener should cup the can over their ear. As long as you keep the string tight, the sound vibrations will travel along it and be easy to hear.

Amazing fact

Sound travels faster near the ground than higher up in the sky. As you go higher, the air gets colder and sound travels through it more slowly. Outside the windows of an aircraft flying at more than 10,000m above the ground, the air temperature can be as low as -60°C. Here, the speed of sound drops to about 294m/sec.

Did you know?

Another scientist who did early experiments with sound was the Irishman Robert Boyle. In 1658 he took a glass bell jar and put it over a ticking watch. With the jar in place he could still hear the watch. He then connected a vacuum pump to the jar and pumped the air out. As the air was removed, the sound of the watch got fainter and fainter until, with all the air pumped out, the watch was silent. It hadn't stopped, though – the second hand was still going round. Boyle had proved that sound does not travel in a vacuum.

Robert Boyle (1627–1691), an Irish chemist and physicist.

Light & Sound

How Loud?

Sounds don't just come in different notes. They come in different volumes as well – from the tiniest whisper to a fire-engine's siren that's so loud it hurts. The loudness of a sound depends on how big the vibrations are. Quiet sounds are small vibrations which carry only a little bit of sound energy through the air. Loud sounds are big vibrations carrying large amounts of energy. The more energy that is carried in the vibrations, the louder the sound will be.

Noise numbers

Loudness is measured in units called decibels, which were named after the American inventor of the telephone, Alexander Graham Bell. What's the quietest sound you can hear? The sound of a ticking watch, or leaves rustling gently in the breeze? Quiet sounds like these measure about 10 to 20 on the decibel scale, which is as low as most people can hear. Some large-eared nocturnal animals can hear sounds even quieter. A barn owl can detect the tread of a mouse on the floor of a barn!

The loudest sounds of all include big explosions and the sound of a space rocket taking off. These may exceed 150dB (decibels). Very loud sounds can be painful and damage your hearing. That's why you automatically put your hands over your ears if a car or fire alarm goes off nearby. Listening to loud sounds for too long – like a personal stereo with the volume turned up too high – can damage your hearing. So, people who work with or near loud noises, such as airport workers and road repairmen, wear ear protectors to muffle the sound and protect their ears.

Louder and louder

Sounds can be made louder, or amplified, using electronic equipment. This is how bands make their music loud enough for everyone to hear at a concert. A microphone picks up the sound and converts it into a series of electrical signals. An amplifier adds electrical energy to make the signals bigger and a loudspeaker converts the signals back into sounds.

Earphones are small loudspeakers.

How Loud?

Try this! Make vibrations

You can experiment with the loudness of sound by making a simple box guitar. You will need an open-topped cardboard box (an empty tissue box or shoe box with the top removed works brilliantly), and a long elastic band. Stretch the elastic band around the box. Now 'twang' the rubber band with your finger. Try twanging it gently and then twang it harder. Can you hear a difference? The loudness of the sound that you produce depends on how hard you pluck the elastic band and how big the sound vibrations are.

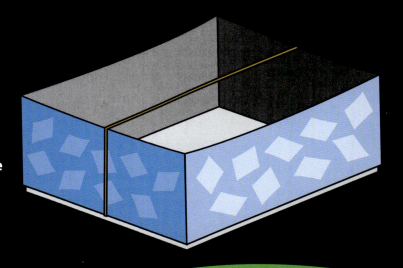

Amazing fact

The loudest sound ever heard on Earth was probably the explosion that blew the volcanic island of Krakatoa, in Indonesia, to bits at 10.00am on 27 August, 1883. It was heard by people up to 5,000km away.

Did you know?

Each time 10 decibels are added on the decibel scale, the loudness is multiplied 10 times. So a 40dB sound is 10 times as loud as a 30dB sound. Here are some typical examples of loudness on the decibel scale.

A watch ticking is about 10dB on the decibel scale.

The sound of a car engine is about 80dB.

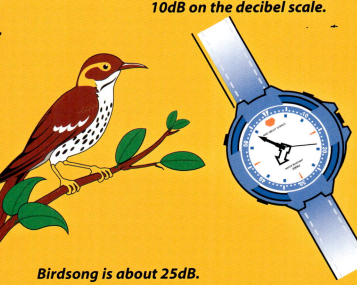

Birdsong is about 25dB.

Light & Sound

High or Low?

The highness or lowness of a sound is known as its pitch. For example, the sound of a whistle is high-pitched, while a bass guitar makes a low-pitched sound. Some animals can hear sounds of a much higher or lower pitch than human beings can. And, just like volume, pitch is all to do with sound vibrations.

Who can hear what?

The pitch of a sound depends on the number of vibrations produced per second, which is called the frequency of the vibration. Pitch is measured in units called hertz where one hertz (1Hz) is equal to one vibration per second. This would be an extremely low sound and human hearing is best at a much higher frequency of about 1,000Hz. However, our hearing gets worse as we get older, and so children are much better at hearing than adults. You can hear sounds from about 20 to 20,000Hz but your parents or grandparents may not be able to hear very high-pitched sounds at all well – and that's why they are always asking you to speak up!

Some animals can hear sounds that are too low in pitch for us to hear. Other animals can hear sounds well above the top of the human hearing range. Bats and dolphins can hear sounds with a pitch as high as a whopping 120,000Hz. Many insects also produce very high-pitched sounds. So what seems to us to be a silent night might really be alive with squeaks and chirrups – we just don't have the right sort of ears to hear them.

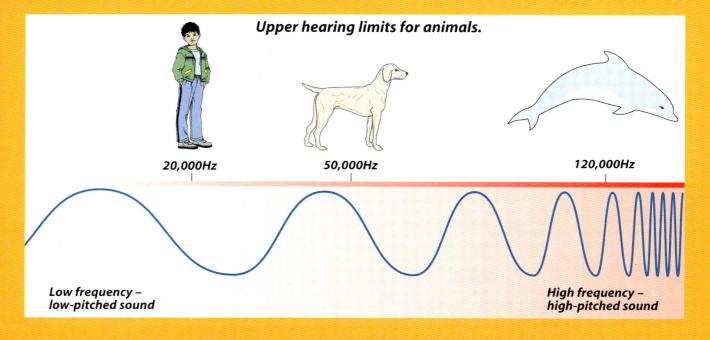

Upper hearing limits for animals.

20,000Hz   50,000Hz   120,000Hz

Low frequency – low-pitched sound

High frequency – high-pitched sound

High or Low?

Try this! Bottle band

Find four or five similar empty glass bottles and put different amounts of water in each. If you blow across the top of the bottle, you will vibrate the column of air inside the bottle and make it produce a sound. The bottle with the most water – and therefore the shortest air column – will produce the highest pitch. Many wind instruments produce notes of different pitch by varying the length of the vibrating column of air inside them.

Try this! Changing pitch

Make a simple box guitar using a box and an elastic band, as on page 23. But this time, add some more elastic bands of different thicknesses. You should find that thicker bands produce lower notes. You can also make the note higher by stretching the elastic band tighter. If you look at a stringed instruments such as a guitar, you'll see that it uses strings of different thicknesses, some stretched tighter than others, to make different notes.

Did you know?

You may have noticed that the sound of a siren on a police car or ambulance seems to stay steady as it comes towards you. But as it goes past, the pitch of the siren falls to a lower note. This is called the Doppler effect, after the Austrian scientist who first explained it in 1842. As the car approaches, the sound waves coming towards you from the siren are bunched slightly together because the car is moving with the sound waves. If the waves are closer together, they have a higher frequency and form a constant high note. As the car moves away from you, the sound waves are stretched farther apart, the frequency drops and the pitch of the sound seems to fall.

Light & Sound

All Ears

Everyone knows what ears are. They're those things on the sides of your head that hold your sunglasses up. Wrong! Those are just the outside bits of your ears. In fact, ears are made up of three parts called the outer, middle and inner ear, and they reach right inside your head to your brain. It's your brain that actually 'hears' sounds, by translating the signals your ears send to it.

How you hear

Ears work by detecting the vibrations that sounds make in the air. The outer ear – which scientists call the pinna – is the part you can see. It is funnel-shaped to catch sounds and send them down a 2–3cm-long tunnel called the ear canal, inside your head. At the end of the ear canal, the vibrations hit your eardrum – a tightly-stretched piece of skin very like the skin of a real drum. The vibrations in the air make the eardrum itself vibrate.

Behind the eardrum is an area called the middle ear, which contains three tiny bones. The first of these, the hammer, is joined to the eardrum. Its other end hinges with the anvil, which is in turn joined to the stirrup. When the eardrum vibrates, the three hinged bones pass on the vibrations to the inner ear. The middle ear is full of air. It is connected to your throat by the Eustachian tube. This is why swallowing helps to make your ears feel better when there's a sudden change in air pressure (like when your plane takes off). When you swallow, air passes up the tube to balance the pressure in your middle ear.

The inner ear is the snail-shaped cochlea, which picks up vibrations from the stirrup bone and turns them into electrical signals. These signals travel along nerves to the brain which then tells us if the telephone is ringing or if the dog is barking. Also attached to the cochlea are three loops called semicircular canals. These tell the brain the position of the head and give us our sense of balance.

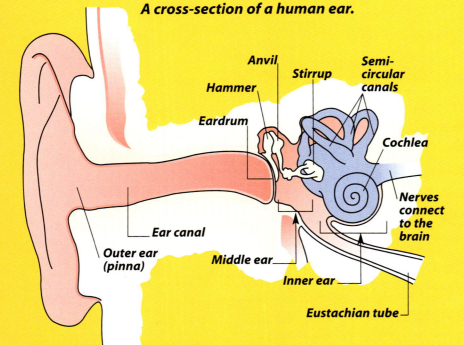

A cross-section of a human ear.

All Ears

Did you know?

While some animals don't have ears (such as sharks and snakes), most animals depend on their hearing for hunting down food, listening out for anything that might be creeping up behind them, and communicating with friends and family. This African serval hunts in the dark. It swivels its ears around to face the direction a sound is coming from so that it can track down prey and pounce with deadly accuracy.

Amazing fact

Spiders don't have ears like us, but they can 'hear' by using special slit sense organs which detect vibrations on their exo-skeleton – the hard outer 'skin' that insects have. Spiders can also pick up vibrations through the air and ground using tiny bristles on their legs and body. These bristles pick up the air movements and buzzing sounds of insects flying up to 30cm away.

Try this! The sound of yourself

When you hear yourself speaking, most of the sound gets to your ears by being conducted along the bones of your skull. To find out what you really sound like to other people, get somebody to make a tape recording of you speaking. When it's played back, you'll be amazed how different you sound.

Try this! Surround sound

Everybody has two ears. So unless a sound comes from directly in front or directly behind us, it arrives at one ear a fraction of a second before it reaches the other. This tiny delay enables us to work out where a sound is coming from. To test this sense, blindfold a friend and sit them in a chair. Get other people to sit or stand around and make noises. Test how well the person can tell where each sound is coming from. Now try this test on different people – are some more accurate than others?

Echo Effects

Like light, sound can bounce! It can be reflected off hard surfaces such as cliffs, buildings or the walls in an empty room, just like light being reflected off a mirror. A reflected sound is called an echo. Since we know the speed of sound, we can use a method called echo sounding to find out how far away an object is by measuring echoes. Some animals use this method too, to spot their enemies or find their prey in the dark.

Bouncing sound

If you stand in a pedestrian underpass or subway and shout out loud, you'll frighten people! But apart from that, you'll also hear your own shout repeated a second or two later. This is an echo, caused by the sound waves being reflected off the walls of the underpass. You can also hear echoes in the countryside if you shout at a cliff or cave wall.

Because we know the speed of sound, echoes can be used to calculate the distance to an object. Echo sounding works best with high-pitched sounds that have a frequency of more than 20,000Hz. This is called ultrasound, as it's too high for humans to hear. Instead, a special receiver is used to pick up sounds as they bounce off objects.

Echo sounding (sometimes called sonar) is used by ships and submarines for measuring distances underwater – such as how deep the sea is. To do this, a ship has an ultrasound transmitter and receiver mounted on its hull. The transmitter sends out a series of ultrasound pulses. They travel through the water, bounce off the sea bed and back to the ship, where they are picked up by the receiver. The depth of water is worked out by measuring the time it takes for the ultrasound to reach the sea bed and bounce back to the ship.

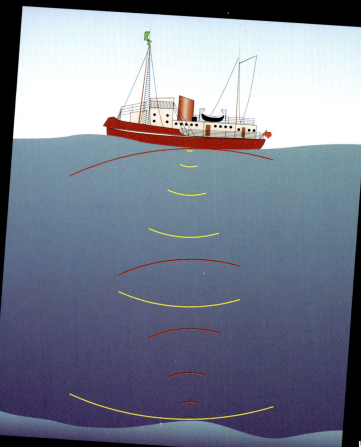

Ships can use echo sounding to check the depth of the water. It's also used to measure distances to icebergs and shoals of fish.

Echo Effects

Did you know?

Some kinds of bats use ultrasound to find their insect prey in the dark. They send out a series of ultrasonic squeaks, and detect any echoes that bounce off insects flying nearby. They then quickly close in on their prey and use their wings to scoop it towards their mouths!

Ultrasound also has medical uses. It can be used to scan a person's body. Some body parts, such as bone, reflect ultrasound better than others, so an ultrasound scan can build up a picture of different tissues in the body.

This is an ultrasound image of an unborn baby in its mother's womb.

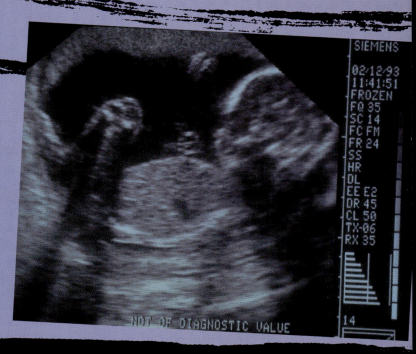

Try this! Making waves

You can imitate sound waves using ripples on the surface of water. You will need a washing-up bowl, water, a small stone and a hard object such as a metal strip. Put 2–3cm of water in the bottom of the bowl. Drop the stone in the middle and see the circular waves rippling outwards. Then stand the metal strip in the bowl. Now, when you drop in the stone, the ripples will be reflected by the strip, just like waves of ultrasound in a sonar echo.

Amazing fact

Dolphins use ultrasound waves to probe the world around them and to communicate with other dolphins. These waves are too high for humans to hear, but they can pass through a metre of mud and can tell dolphins the difference between solid and hollow objects, such as between rocks and fish.

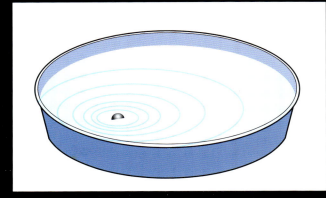
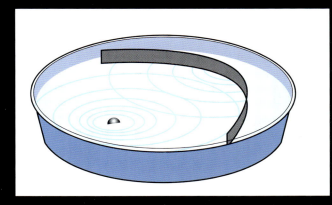

Light & Sound

Making Waves

As you know, light and sound are both forms of energy. They also have something else in common – they both travel as waves. But we can't see them like other familiar kinds of waves, such as ripples on a pond after you throw in a stone or waves of sea-water rolling onto a beach.

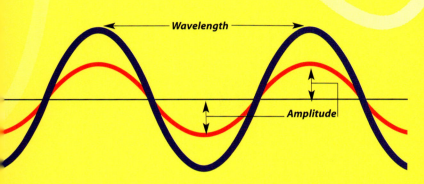

What are waves?

A wave happens when something moves up and down. These regular up-and-down movements can carry energy from one place to another. All waves have a series of peaks and troughs (that look like a row of hills and valleys). The distance between any two neighbouring peaks (or troughs) is the wavelength. Waves with a short wavelength have a high frequency, which means that a lot of waves pass in one second. Light has an extremely short wavelength and travels at a mind-boggling 300,000km/sec – nothing travels faster!

The strength of a wave is measured by its amplitude, which is the height of the wave above its average position. The amplitude lets you know how much energy the wave is carrying, so light waves with a large amplitude are very bright. Sound waves with a high amplitude are very loud.

Try this! Wave movement

When a wave moves through a material – like a sound wave travelling through air – the material itself does not move along with the wave. You can see this with waves on water. You'll need a cork, some pebbles and a pond. Throw the cork into the pond. Next throw a pebble near to the floating cork. As the water waves, or ripples, travel past the cork, the cork just bobs up and down. It does not travel along with the ripples.

Amazing fact

The largest sea waves are called tidal waves, or tsunami. Earthquakes and volcanic eruptions on the seabed cause them. The largest ever recorded was 525m high and rushed across a bay in Alaska at a speed of 160km/h.

Glossary

Amplitude
The height of a wave; the distance a wave moves from its average position.

Concave
Curving inwards.

Convex
Curving outwards.

Echo
A sound heard for the second time after it bounces off a distant object.

Frequency
For any wave motion, the number of vibrations or waves that pass in one second.

Lens
A piece of curved and polished glass or plastic, used to bend (refract) light.

Light
A type of energy that we can see, produced mainly by very hot objects such as the Sun or the filament of an electric light bulb.

Opaque
Describing a material that will not let light pass through it.

Pitch
In sound, the highness or lowness of a note, measured by the sound's frequency.

Prism
A triangular block of glass that can split white light into a spectrum.

Reflection
The change in the direction of light when it bounces off a mirror.

Refraction
The change in the direction of light when it passes from one transparent material into another.

Shadow
An area to which light rays are blocked by something opaque.

Sound
A type of energy produced by vibrating objects and taking the form of waves in air or another material.

Spectrum
A range of colours, including the colours of the rainbow, produced when a prism splits up white light.

Transparent
Describing a material that lets light pass through it.

Vibration
Rapid up-and-down or side-to-side movements of an object, such as the skin of a drum or the string of a guitar being played.

Wave
A regularly repeating motion, in a medium (such as air or water) or in space, which carries energy.

Wavelength
For any wave motion, the distance between the crests (or troughs) of two neighbouring waves.

Index

A
aircraft *19, 21*
amplitude *31*
animals *22, 24, 27, 28–9*

B
bats *24, 29*
Bell, Alexander Graham *22*
bioluminescence *5*
blind spot, eye *16*
Boyle, Robert *21*
brain *14–15, 16–17, 26*

C
cameras *14, 17*
candles *4*
colours *12–13, 15*
concave *8, 11, 31*
convex *8, 11, 31*

D
decibels *22, 23*
Derham, William *20*
dolphins *24, 28, 29*
Doppler effect *25*

E
ears *22, 26–7*
echo sounding *28*
echoes *28–9, 31*
eclipses *7*
electricity *4*
eyes *5, 8, 14–17*

F
filters, colour *13*
frequency *24, 25, 31*

G
glass *6, 9, 10–11*

H
hearing *22, 24, 26–7*
heat energy *4*
hertz *24*

I
illusions *16–17*
insects *15, 24, 27*

L
lamps *4*
Leeuwenhoek, Anton van *11*
lenses *10–11, 14, 17, 31*
light bulbs *4*
loudness *22–3*
luminescence *5*

M
magnifying glasses *11, 14*
microscopes *11*

mirrors *6, 8–9, 13*
Moon *7, 9*
music *18, 19, 22*

N
Newton, Isaac *12*
night *6*
noise *18*

O
oil lamps *4*
opaque objects *6, 31*
optical illusions *16–17*

P
periscopes *9*
phosphors *4*
photosynthesis *4*
pitch *24–5, 31*
plants *4*
prisms *12, 31*

R
rainbows *12–13*
reflections *8–9, 31*
refraction *10, 12, 31*
retina *14, 15, 16*

S
shadows *6–7, 31*
sonar *28*
sonic booms *19*

sound waves *18–21, 25, 28–30*
spectrum *12–13, 31*
speed of light *5*
speed of sound *5, 20–1, 28*
spiders *27*
stars *11*
Sun *4–7*
sundials *7*
sunlight *4–7, 12*

T
telescopes *11*
television *4, 13, 17*
3-D vision *15*
transparent objects *6, 10, 31*

U
ultrasound *28–9*
ultraviolet light *15*

V
vacuums *21*
vibrations, sound *18–23, 31*

W
water *10, 12, 13, 20, 28*
wavelength *31*
waves *18–21, 25, 28–31*